ANCIENT INDIA

ANCIENT CIVILIZATIONS IN REVIEW

By Seth Lynch

Enslow Publishing

Please visit our website, www.enslow.com. For a free color catalog of all our high-quality books, call toll free 1-800-398-2504 or fax 1-877-980-4454.

Library of Congress Cataloging-in-Publication Data
Names: Lynch, Seth, author.
Title: Ancient India / Seth Lynch.
Description: Buffalo, New York : Enslow Publishing, [2025] | Series: Ancient civilizations in review | Includes index.
Identifiers: LCCN 2024023247 | ISBN 9781978542822 (library binding) | ISBN 9781978542815 (paperback) | ISBN 9781978542839 (ebook)
Subjects: LCSH: India–History–Juvenile literature. | India–Civilization–Juvenile literature.
Classification: LCC DS436 .L96 2025 | DDC 934–dc23/eng/20240523
LC record available at https://lccn.loc.gov/2024023247
Published in 2025 by
Enslow Publishing
2544 Clinton Street
Buffalo, NY 14224

Portions of this work were originally authored by Daniel R. Faust and published as *Ancient India*. All new material this edition authored by Seth Lynch.

Designer: Leslie Taylor
Editor: Kristen Nelson

Photo credits: Cover (main photo) ImagesofIndia/Shutterstock, (Buddha) NARONGRIT LOKOOLPRAKIT/Shutterstock.com, (back cover dancer) ShaikhMeraj/Shutterstock.com; Cover and series art (vintage map) Andrey_Kuzmin/Shutterstock.com (brush strokes) ozzichka/Shutterstock.com, (font) MagicPics/Shutterstock.com; p. 5 Bezruk/Shutterstock.com; p. 7 khlongwangchao/Shutterstock.com; p. 8 (plate) shozib ali brohi, (animal figurine) shozib ali brohi/Shutterstock.com; p. 9 TripDeeDee Photo/Shutterstock.com; p. 10 tete_escape/Shutterstock.com; p. 11 doctor_k/Shutterstock.com; p. 13 WESTOCK PRODUCTIONS/Shutterstock.com; p. 14 Roshp/Shutterstock.com; p. 15 Nila Newsom/Shutterstock.com; p. 17 (all images) Shutterstock AI Generator/Shutterstock.com; p. 19 Dmitrii Sakharov/Shutterstock.com; p. 21 travelwild/Shutterstock.com; p. 23 (relief map) zelvan/Shutterstock.com, (shaded area) Avantiputra7/File:Maurya Empire, c.250 BCE 2.png_commons.wikimedia.org; p. 25 Jen/File:Vishnu sculpture.jpg_commons.wikimedia.org; p. 27 Arjunullas/ File:Cheraman Juma Palli.jpg_commons.wikimedia.org; p. 29 sladkozaponi/Shutterstock.com.

Printed in the United States of America

CPSIA compliance information: Batch #CWENS25: For further information, contact Enslow Publishing at 1-800-398-2504.

CONTENTS

Words in the glossary appear in **bold** the first time they are used in the text.

The Great Subcontinent

Today, the Indian subcontinent is home to the countries of India, Bangladesh, and Pakistan, among others. It's also where some of the world's oldest civilizations began! Human history in ancient India starts before 7000 BCE when people began to farm near the Indus River.

LEARN MORE

Ancient means very old or having to do with something that happened long ago.

GHANISTAN
CHINA
Indus River
Pakistan
NEPAL
BHUTAN
Bangledesh
INDIA
MYANMAR
present-day
Indian subcontinent
BAY OF BENGAL
ARABIAN SEA
SRI LANKA

Indus Valley Civilization

Early people in India needed the river's water to drink, cook, and water their fields. Over time, they built villages and raised goats, sheep, and cows. These villages grew into larger cities. Over time, these cities grew to be the Indus Valley civilization.

LEARN MORE

The yearly Indus River floods made the soil around it good for farming.

Indus River

The Indus Valley civilization rose around 2500 BCE. Two of its largest cities were Mohenjo-daro and Harappa. These cities were advanced for their time. They had well-planned streets, indoor bathrooms, and sewer systems that ran throughout the city.

plate and figure from Mohenjo-daro

LEARN MORE

The remains of Harappa and Mohenjo-daro were discovered in the early 1920s. Historians have studied these cities to learn more about ancient India.

remains of Mohenjo-daro

One important crop of the Indus Valley civilization was cotton. Cotton was brought to cities and made into cloth. The cloth was a key trade good. It's likely the Indus Valley civilization traded with peoples in Southern India, Mesopotamia, and elsewhere.

indigo-dyed cloth

LEARN MORE

Indigo, a bright blue dye, is also thought to come from India. The Greeks called this blue color *indikon*, which means "from India."

indigo dye

The Vedic Period

The Indus Valley civilization was failing by 1700 BCE. Soon after, people sometimes called the Indo-Aryans arrived in ancient India. This time is called the Vedic Period. It's called "Vedic" after the Vedas, books important to Hinduism written during this time.

LEARN MORE

It's not known why the Indus Valley civilization failed. It may have been because of a change in the **climate** or an **invasion** from the west.

The Holy
Vedas
Rig Veda
Yajur Veda
Sama Veda
Atharva Veda

Most of what we know about ancient India comes from writings of the Vedic Period. These writings are in a language called Sanskrit. Two long pieces of writing still studied today—the *Ramayana* and the *Mahabharata*—were also written in this language.

the *Ramayana*

LEARN MORE

Sanskrit is one of the languages of India. You can see parts of Sanskrit in other languages throughout Southeast Asia.

Sanskrit

The Caste System

Over time, beliefs held in the Vedic Period would become Hinduism. One belief, the caste system, rose around 1500 BCE. It sorted the people of India into four main classes based on their work and **religious** duty.

LEARN MORE

People in the highest caste had the most money and power. People were born into their caste and it was hard to move to a higher caste.

HINDU CASTE SYSTEM

Brahmans
priests, teachers

Kshatriyas
warriors (or fighters), rulers

Vaishyas
shopkeepers, traders, farmers

Shudras
farmers, laborers

Buddhism

Buddhism is another large religion that began in ancient India. Buddhism is based on the teachings of a man named Siddhartha Gautama. Gautama was a prince from a kingdom in northeast India. He became the first Buddha, or "**enlightened** one."

LEARN MORE

Buddhism spread throughout Asia. It changed the beliefs and ways of life of people in other countries such as China, Japan, and Korea.

Buddha statue, Phuket, Thailand

Divided Power

Around 700 BCE, 16 kingdoms, or mahajanapadas, began to rise in the Ganges River valley. Several of these 16 kingdoms fought for control over the area. The state of Magadha gained power by taking over other mahajanapadas.

LEARN MORE

"Mahajanapada" means great state or kingdom.

Ganges River

INVASIONS

The Persian Empire invaded northern India during the 500s BCE. Then, as Alexander the Great took over the lands of the Persian Empire, he led troops to conquer India in 327 BCE. However, he died in 323 BCE. Soon after, the Mauryan Empire rose to power.

LEARN MORE

The Mauryan Empire lasted until about 185 BCE. At its height, it controlled most of the Indian subcontinent.

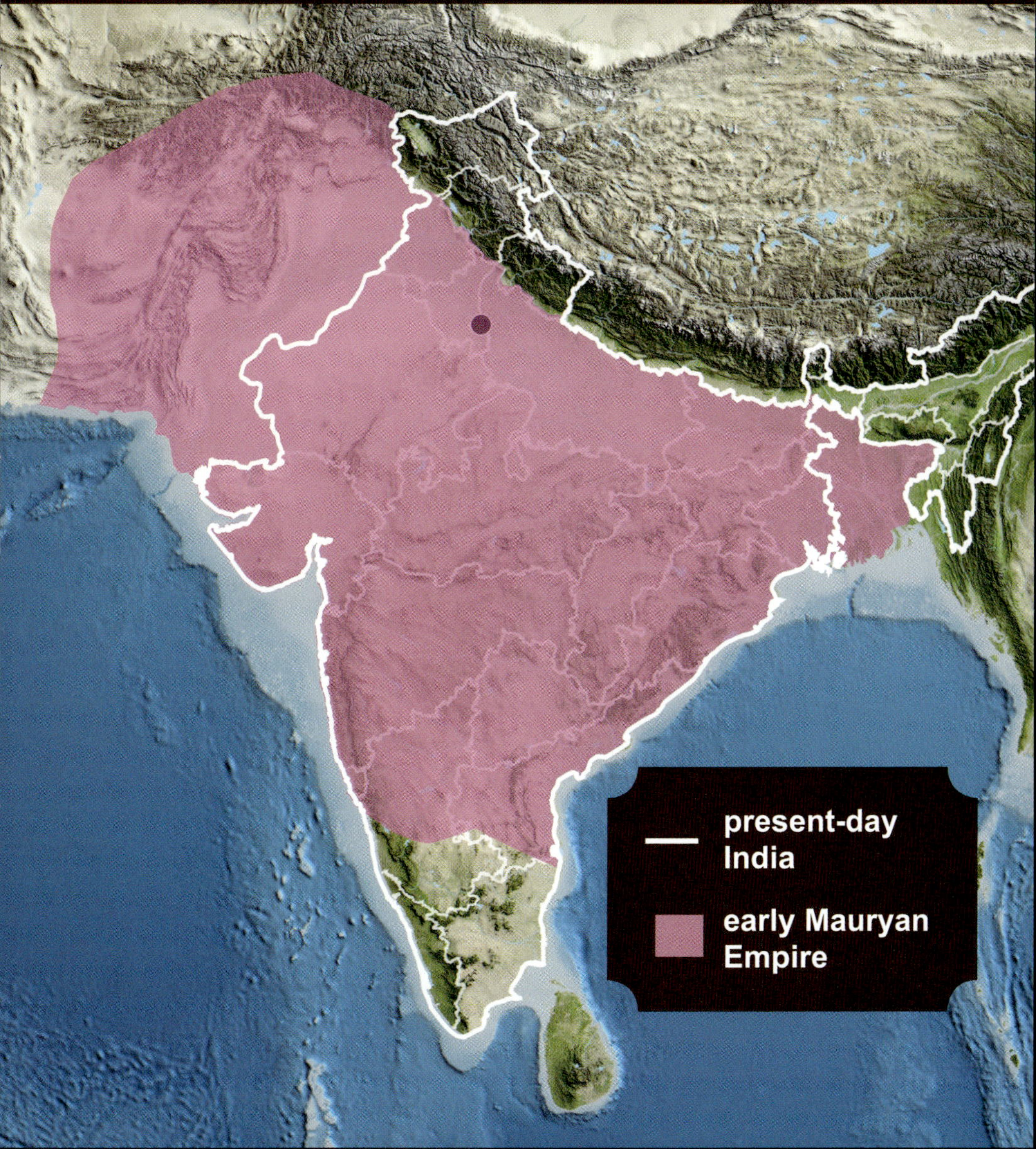
present-day
India
early Mauryan
Empire

The Gupta Dynasty

The next big empire in India did not come to power until about 320 CE. The Gupta dynasty controlled northern India and present-day Bangladesh and Pakistan. During this **dynasty**, work in the arts, writing, and music grew.

LEARN MORE

Art from this time often had to do with Hinduism.

Hindu art,
Gupta dynasty

Muslim Control

Around the year 550, the Gupta dynasty fell. Its lands broke apart into smaller kingdoms. Starting around the year 900, Muslims began to take over India piece by piece. India would be under the control of other countries until the mid-20th century.

LEARN MORE

Muslims are followers of the religion Islam. They pray five times each day and gather at religious houses called mosques.

oldest mosque in India

Greater Influence

Ideas and inventions from ancient India are still around today! Ancient Indians invented rulers for measuring, scales for weighing, and the game of chess. Hindu writings from around 700 CE even say how long it took Earth to circle the sun almost perfectly!

LEARN MORE

There are 1.4 billion people in India today whose lives have been shaped by their subcontinent's ancient history!

present-day Mumbai, India

Timeline of Ancient India

c. 7000 BCE......... People begin farming by the Indus River.

c. 2500–1700 BCE...... The Indus Valley civilization rises.

c. 1500 BCE..............Indo-Aryans arrive in ancient India.

c. 700 BCE........ Sixteen mahajanapadas come to power in northeast India.

c. 500s BCE............The Persian Empire invades northern India.

327 BCE..................Alexander the Great conquers parts of India.

321–185 BCE........ The Mauryan Empire controls much of the subcontinent of India.

c. 320–550 CE ....The Gupta dynasty holds power.

c. 900 CE.................. Muslims begin to take over parts of India.

GLOSSARY

civilization: Organized society with written records and laws.

climate: The average weather of a place.

conquer: To take by force.

dynasty: A line of rulers who belong to a single family.

empire: A large area of land under the control of a single ruler.

enlightened: Having an open mind and showing a good understanding of how people should be treated.

Hinduism: A major religion that began in ancient India. Hindus honor many gods and believe that after death a person returns to life in a different form.

invasion: The entering of a place to take it over.

priest: A leader in some religions.

religious: Having to do with religion, or a faith with a set of beliefs.

sewer system: Underground pipes that are used to carry away water and waste matter.

subcontinent: A large area of land that is a part of one of Earth's seven major landmasses (North America, South America, Europe, Asia, Africa, Australia, and Antarctica).

FOR MORE INFORMATION

BOOKS

Hyde, Natalie. *Focus on India.* St. Catharines, ON, Canada: Crabtree Publishing, 2025.

Simons, Lisa M. Bolt. *Super Surprising Trivia About Ancient Civilizations.* North Mankato, MN: Capstone Press, 2024.

WEBSITE

History for Kids: Ancient Indian Daily Life
https://www.historyforkids.net/ancient-indian-daily-life-for-kids.html
Read about all parts of ancient Indian life here.

INDEX